SKJC

21st Century
Basic Skills
Library

WHAT DO PEOPLE DO IN SPRING?

by Jenna Lee Gleisner

Cherry Lake Publishing • Ann Arbor, Michigan

1

Published in the United States of America
by Cherry Lake Publishing
Ann Arbor, Michigan
www.cherrylakepublishing.com

Consultant: Marla Conn, ReadAbility, Inc.

Photo Credits: Patrick Foto/Shutterstock Images, Cover, Title; Jaroslava V/Shutterstock Images, 4; Samuel Borges Photography/Shutterstock Images, 6; Warren Goldswain/Shutterstock Images, 8; Shutterstock Images, 10, 12, 16, 18, 20; wavebreakmedia/Shutterstock Images, 14

Library of Congress Cataloging-in-Publication Data
Gleisner, Jenna Lee.
  What do people do in spring? / by Jenna Lee Gleisner.
     pages cm. -- (Let's look at spring)
  Audience: 5-7.
  Audience: K to grade 3.
  Includes index.
  ISBN 978-1-62431-661-6 (hardcover) -- ISBN 978-1-62431-688-3 (pbk.) -- ISBN 978-1-62431-715-6 (pdf) -- ISBN 978-1-62431-742-2 (hosted ebook)
  1. Spring--Juvenile literature. I. Title.

  QH637.5.G54 2013
  508.2--dc23

                        2013029055

Cherry Lake Publishing would like to acknowledge the work of The Partnership for 21st Century Skills.
Please visit www.p21.org for more information.

Printed in the United States of America
Corporate Graphics Inc.
January 2014

TABLE OF CONTENTS

5   **Spring Changes**

11 **Plants**

17 **Gardens**

21 **School Ends**

22 Find Out More

22 Glossary

23 Home and School Connection

24 Index

24 About the Author

Spring Changes

Spring is here. The **temperature** rises. Weather gets warmer.

Ria feels it is warmer. She reads her book outside.

People spend more time outside. Ray walks his dog.

What Do You See?

What kind of flower do you see?

Plants

Plants and flowers begin to grow. People enjoy the bright colors.

What Do You See?

What color is the flower?

12

Bo smells flowers at the park.
He picks one to take home.

People celebrate **Arbor Day** and **Earth Day** in spring. We learn about and care for Earth.

What Do You See?

How many tomatoes do you see?

Gardens

People plant gardens.
Will **tends** his vegetables
all spring.

18

Kate plants a flower garden.
She waters it each morning.

School Ends

The school year ends in spring.
Summer is almost here!

Find Out More

BOOK

Rissman, Rebecca. *Seasons*. Chicago: Capstone Raintree, 2014.

WEB SITE

Tree House Weather Kids
www.urbanext.illinois.edu/treehouse/index.cfm
Learn what causes seasons and changes in temperature.

Glossary

Arbor Day (AHR-bur day) a special day for planting trees

Earth Day (URTH day) a special day for learning about and caring for our Earth

temperature (TEM-pur-uh-chur) how hot or cold something is

tend (TEND) to take care of

Home and School Connection

Use this list of words from the book to help your child become a better reader. Word games and writing activities can help beginning readers reinforce literacy skills.

book	home	school	walks
celebrate	morning	spring	warmer
colors	outside	summer	weather
dog	park	temperature	year
flowers	people	tends	
gardens	plants	time	
grow	reads	vegetables	

What Do You See?

What Do You See? is a feature paired with select photos in this book. It encourages young readers to interact with visual images in order to build the ability to integrate content in various media formats.

You can help your child further evaluate photos in this book with additional activities. Look at the images in the book without the What Do You See? feature. Ask your child to point out one detail in each image, such as a color, time of day, animal, or setting.

Index

Arbor Day, 15

Earth Day, 15

flowers, 11, 13, 19

garden, 17, 19

outside, 7, 9

plants, 11, 17, 19

school, 21
summer, 21

temperature, 5

vegetables, 17

weather, 5

About the Author

Jenna Lee Gleisner is an editor and author who lives in Minnesota. She likes to plant flowers and take her dog for walks in spring!